What To Expect When Your Daughter Hits Double Digits

A Step by Step Guide to Survive and Thrive Through the Teenage Years

Andrea Nelson Lewis

ISBN 1500741965
ISBN 13: 9781500741969

Printed in USA by CreateSpace

Editor: Allyson M. Deese at www.allysonmdeese.com

Cover Illustrator: Mary Caroline Holland at mchollandartwork@gmail.com

Photographer: Monifa Basdeo of Picture Perfect at www.facebook.com/p3photography08

Dedication

This book is dedicated to my mother Betty Reeves Nelson Calhoun who provided the best example of motherhood by raising countless teenage girls.

Thanks to my husband Brian who was a constant partner in raising our daughter Addison.

Many thanks go to several friends and family (Addison, Allison, Angela, Brian, Chris, Eryn, Jasmine, John, Karen, Kimberly, Larry, Madison, Molly, Satima, Savannah, Shannon, and Sonya) who reviewed my manuscript and or provided actual experiences and insights. A special thanks to Janet Smith Dozier for her relentless and everlasting support. This book could not have been published without their input.

Table of Contents

Dedication iii

Table of Contents v

Preface vii

Foreword ix

Introduction xi

Chapter One: What Should I Expect? 1

Chapter Two: What Happened to My Little Princess? 11

Chapter Three: Pushing Boundaries 15

Chapter Four: The Mother / Daughter Debate 23

Chapter Five: Daddy Dearest 29

Chapter Six: The Teen Daughter's Perspective 35

Chapter Seven: Coping Mechanisms 43

Chapter Eight: Moving Forward and Looking Back 51

Preface

The book provides a guide to not only survive, but thrive through the often painful metamorphosis of teenage girls. The metamorphosis can begin before your daughter hits the teenage years hence the reference to double digits.

The book grew out of the incessant need of parents' that required relentless searches and comparison of friends' experiences and doctors' notes to understand if their teen's actions and parental responses were normal. In the past, children were raised by a community of family and neighbors who had past experiences and knowledge. Today, families move and are more transitory so the child rearing knowledge is lost or not shared. This book fills in the gap and compiles experience and knowledge in one place.

The book is for *you* and every person who frequently interact with, and influence teenage girls such as parents, aunts, uncles, guardians, grandparents, clergy, and teachers. Kudos to you for taking this step to understand the ever-changing mind of girls approaching or in the teen years. Here is your guide on what to expect during and how to navigate through this phase including life examples known as **Teen Moments** from current teen girls and young women who recently left that stage of their life. Additional advice from these teen girls and their parents is listed in the Question and Answer session in the chapter *Moving Forward and Looking Back.*

Foreword

There is no magic book filled with guaranteed solutions for successful parenting. Scholars, behaviorists, and experts of the human mind have yet to present us with the set of guidelines that will help us raise the perfect child. After all, no two boys or girls are exactly alike. For each child is an individual created with a mind of his or her own overflowing with thoughts, ideas, opinions, preferences and so much more. Parents can only give it their best shot, whisper a prayer, and hope for the best. Honestly, those of us who have been blessed with children are raising them through the process of trial and error. Some of us have been lucky, while others have crashed and burned.

Andrea Nelson Lewis can be considered as one of the many winners in the sport we call parenthood. It's a sport alright, because often times it's the kiddies versus the folks. In the best case scenario, we're all tied up at the end of the game without the possibility of a definitive winner. That situation is a hell of a lot better than the parents taking a brutal beating on the score board. That usually means that the child gets away with violating a major rule which has a negative impact on the entire family, and the parents are expected to clean up the mess. Ultimately, that's a loss for both parent(s) and child(ren).

As a performance mother, Andrea has experienced a whole other side of parenting. In addition to fulfilling the traditional duties of a working wife and mother, there was this amazing talent that she was required to nurture and manage. Her daughter's God-given gift to dance landed Andrea in the middle of a world filled with stress and pressure. There were endless strenuous rehearsals, fierce competitions, image issues, and constant struggles to maintain one's sanity. Who said it was easy to be a dance mom? Everyone wants to win. For most, losing is not an option. But the approach to succeeding in the dance world is different for each young dancer and their parent. The overall process can be a life-changing experience. For Andrea Nelson Lewis, it was indeed. In fact, it was as challenging as earning her dual degrees in chemical engineering and pulp and paper technology from North

Carolina State University and an executive masters of business from Emory University. During her years and extensive involvement as a dance mom, she encountered countless young dancers, teenage girls, as well as their parents and siblings. Through observation and interaction, she soaked in an abundance of information, both good and bad. She witnessed positive and negative behaviors and reactions worthy of inclusion into her parenting playbook. Thankfully, Andrea, her husband Brian, and their daughter Addison survived and thrived through the normal side of growing up and mastered the world of competitive dancing. In this book she will share with you their journey of just how they made it work, including a set of guidelines to achieve success. After all, as Andrea reminds us, "Parenting is an art and not a science of one problem and one solution."

Allison Randall Berewa AKA Honey, author
*Secrets of Love and Redemption
*Deranged Love & Deranged Love 2 Twisted Faith
*Winter Wonder Man, a short story featured in the anthology A Man for Every Season

Introduction

A teenage girl is an individual like none other.
Her mercurial temperament waxes and wanes,
With hormones, comparisons, or struggles with mother,
Or nothing at all will give her pain.
On her journey to self-awareness and individuality,
Mistakes and memories pave her path.
Don't worry, she will find her niche along with your wrath.
Be loving, flexible, patient, and kind,
Don't forget rules, structure, and stated expectations.
That tough love must rule her nation.
Guide with communication, consequences, and honesty,
She won't appreciate your wisdom of what must be.
And as she matures, your intellect wises, too
She comes into her own now appreciating her and you. ☺

Chapter One: What Should I Expect?

As we know, during puberty there are physical, outward cues reminding us blatantly that our little girl won't be little for much longer. She's getting taller, breasts are budding, hair and acne are popping up all over, menstruation starts, and even her voice is lowering...yes, girl's voices lower too.

These outward changes are easier to accommodate with purchases of items. Whether the purchase is for more clothes to accommodate the growth, shaving and depilatory utensils to manage the hair, acne solutions to fight the dreaded bumps, and feminine products to control the monthly flow, parents often have this feeling of "Oh No! What's happening to my little girl and what am I supposed to do?" Here are some steps to put you on the right road to manage the physical changes.

Step 1: Relax. This is a normal process that happens to every girl. The process like any other takes time and will cause a few bumps in the road, but how you respond is infectious and will lay the groundwork for your daughter's response.

Step 2: Communicate. Talk about what is going on, what to expect, and how she may feel. Remember that communication is not a one-time deal, but requires series of discussions before some of the ideas stick. Remember when she was a baby, you had to introduce a food several times before she liked or at least tolerated it. The same goes for communication especially given that various physical changes will keep occurring and the talks will have to change depending on the new aspect of teen hood. Don't sound preachy, but do include her feelings by saying, "What do you think or how do you feel about this?" Communication is a *two way* street.

Hormone Overload – A Roller Coaster of Emotions:

So we have established that the physical changes may be easier handled with the purchase of items. But what about managing the hormones, the inner changes that can't be seen in the mirror, you know the genesis of the barrage of physical changes as well as emotional activity? Hormones happen. Point blank. Period. It's no getting around them. To manage the hormones, here is what you and daughter can do. Remember that most of the management lies with you - the parent, grandparent, or guardian. Your daughter has a vested interest here and can also keep the hormones in check. You can help her by getting her to do the following as you set the guidelines.

Of course this *may not* be easy, since what you say is probably the *last* thing that she wants to do, but sometimes you can't give choices at home. Realize that she will do what she wants, and that you no longer have control of her actions when she is out of your sight. However, you can facilitate the balance by laying the foundation at home. You do the following and request that your daughter does also.

> *Step 1: Set expectations.* Talk with your daughter and let her know that the mood swings she is experiencing are real. Let her know that the hormone stuff that is going on in her body is expected, but you need some ground rules. You want her to control her actions, respect herself and others, and follow the house rules. Yes, this may be a hard time for her and everyone *will* get through this.

> *Step 2: Be an example.* Demonstrate the behavior that you want to see in her. This is not easy and may cause a reset of the family patterns, but it is necessary for you, the family, and teen daughter to build a harmonious environment.

Step 3: Relax and Choose: Try not to overreact to every situation that comes up. When interesting situations come up, speak calmly, but with authority because after all - YOU are the parent. Teen daughters can be melodramatic so they don't need you to feed into that behavior. Just think through the questions below and choose to relax and how and if you will respond.

Remember when she wanted to wear that pink tutu and cowboy boots with a sweater during the summer (or whatever outfit or ragged stuffed animal that she wanted to carry that just didn't fit into your idea of right) and you let her? These questions will help you choose whether to respond. Remember to RELAX.

- Is this a battle worth fighting? The answer maybe "No" or "Yes" or "Yes, but at a later time."
- Is someone's safety at risk and will not handling this lead to something bigger?
- Does this decision impact future decisions?

Sometimes she just wants to get attention so realize she may be testing you or pushing her boundaries.

Step 4: Eat healthy: Make healthy purchases to fill your refrigerator and pantry. The closest the food is to its original state, the better. A good rule of thumb is if the food has a parent (animal or plant) then you are doing pretty well. For example Cheese Puffs, doesn't have a parent, but cheese does. Another example is potato chips don't have a parent (there are no potato chips plants), but potatoes do. Eat healthy: Potato chips and sodas aren't considered a part of any food group. You know the deal and have heard this before:

- ***Fruits and Veggies:*** eat four to six servings (a serving size for you is the amount of food that can fit in the palm of your hand) of fruit and vegetables a day. Although you can get servings from fruit and vegetable drinks including orange juice, there are more nutritional benefits with the actual fruit including higher fiber content to keep you regular and the added benefit of being more economical.

- **_Fluids:_** Drink plenty of fluids especially water. The typical amount of fluid needed for you depends on your weight. Take your weight in pounds (let's say 120 lbs.) and divide by two to get the number of ounces (120 / 2 = 60 oz.) of fluid you need per day. Those stimulants like energy drinks and coffee don't really count. However, there are many studies that say coffee and its caffeine may help. You just need to look at the current studies and see which ones are relevant to you. Last, as a parent, you have a God-given intuition that will lead you in the right direction.

- **_Location_**: Eating at home with meals that you have prepared usually provides the benefits of healthier food with less calories and fat, more economical options, and a venue to communicate about your daughter's day and family discussions. You can still eat out and enjoy each other just remember that at home time is invaluable.

Step 5: Exercise. Yes, I know that you may not want to hear this, but exercise is so important to balancing endorphin hormones. These hormones that produce pain killing and happy feelings are found naturally in the body and will increase when exercising. Choose exercise that is fun like playing volleyball or walking. Note that the exercise does not have to be vigorous like running a marathon, or expensive like some organized sports that are typical of our daughter's generation; instead, just ensure you and your daughter do about twenty to thirty minutes of exercise four to five times a week to balance the hormones.

Step 6: Sleep Well. Make sure that she gets the appropriate amount of sleep (averaging from eight to nine hours). Teenagers' sleep patterns shift to going to bed later around 11 pm so remember to get an eight hour night of sleep your teen must adjust her schedule to get the requisite amount of sleep.

Without this rest, she can revert to the terrible two year old stage that has tantrums of crying, but with the added effects of shouting, yelling, rolling eyes, being impatient, and even perhaps the silent treatment. The lack of sleep can also impact eating habits (overeating), wanting to use stimulants like caffeine or energy drinks to stay awake or sleep aids to fall asleep, acne (*oh no!*) and her attentiveness at school. When you have a question about what to do to help her sleep, go natural like playing white noise music, taking a bath, and restricting stimulating / interactive activities like the Social Media / games/ cell phones / computers, etc. at least one hour before sleep. Again, think back to when she was a toddler and bring back those old methods you used then, but in a more mature state.

Step 7: Be consistent: It is not easy to start a habit of how you will handle your teenage daughter's emotional outbursts or withdrawal. But this is our job as parents / guardians. So before you can succeed at anything, you need a plan. So use this book to consistently prepare, plan, and respond to this phase of her life. Be consistent with your rules and consequences (rewards and punishments).

A Teen Moment: "Wow, I noticed so many changes… some good and some not so good. I've always been an emotional person but I noticed that as I got older my emotions got worse especially in high school."

Birds of a Feather – Friends Today and Not Tomorrow

Along with the mercurial temperament that your daughter exudes in a moment's notice, you will also note that her taste in friends vary just as much.

One day she may have fifty best friends and another day she'll have none. So how should a parent or guardian navigate this quagmire of friendship?

> ***Step 1: Encourage Mingling.*** Let her know that finding your true friends is like finding your true self. How do you know what friends are right for you when you are still trying to figure out who you are? So… encourage her to mingle and go in and out of several groups. Have her do the following:
>
> - ***First:*** Find friends with interests that she currently has. This could be people who do or do not like fashion, sports, same socioeconomic status, race, etc. If that doesn't work, then continue on to step two.
>
> - ***Second:*** Find friends who are like she wants to be or who do the things that she wants to do. Example: if she wants to be a better student and academics are important to her, have her seek out these type of people, groups, or societies that they frequent. If she likes skating, but has never tried it, then she should begin hanging out with people or where people with those tendencies hang. Does she like religion? Have her find a group that seeks a higher being.
>
> - ***Third:*** As her interests change and she finds out more of what she does and does not like, then her friends that she hangs out with should change. Has she heard the saying that friends outgrow friends? It doesn't mean that she thinks less of a person or that she is superior or inferior, it only means that she is no longer as similar to her as she once was. Remind her, that both she and her friends are changing so they could have outgrown her similarly.
>
> ***Step 2: Encourage Authenticity.*** Tell them to be the individual that they are. Remind them that an original is worth more than a copy.
>
> - ***Be Herself:*** Once she has a group (remember that it may change tomorrow), tell her don't try to fit in, just be who

she is. True friends won't try to change her. They may give her pointers on ways to be a better person (they can also lead her down the wrong path). Tell her to decide if their advice is good or bad and what the consequences are of accepting their advice. If the advice means she has to hide who she is, brings trouble, or is illegal, then she may want to rethink this group of friends.

Step 3: Encourage Flexibility. Just like your daughter's body and mind is changing, so is her personality. So if her personality and likes / dislikes have changed significantly, her group of friends or acquaintances may need to change, too. Remind her that this is normal so adjust friendships as she changes. Nothing is wrong with this. Tell her to keep the transitions cool, making no big deal out of it. Remind her to:

• **_Adjust if needed:_** So...now that she has a group to call her friends, have her figure out if this is working for her. Now that she knows them better, does what they say or do offend her or others? Would she like her teachers or parents to see her with them or what they do privately? Does this group encourage her to be a better person or make her want to reach new heights? Is it just fun to be with them or is it tiring and causes strain? Based on her answers to the questions, she should know if they are the group for her or if she should find another group of friends.

Step 4: Engage don't dictate: Parents, you are not to dictate what friends (unless these friends can cause physical, emotional, or legal harm) you want her to have. Instead challenge her to figure it out on her own by asking her questions (not all at once, but over several conversations and weeks / months) in non-judgmental ways. For example, what do you like to do? Do your friends share these experiences / likes / dislikes? What do you and your friends want to do in the future? What activities are you and your friends in together? You could say depending on your daughter's answers – Seems like you guys share a lot in common. Wow, your friends are an eclectic mix. It's nice to have friends with different perspectives to understand differences. It seems like your friends have found a unique way to express themselves. What do you think of your / their decisions?

Notes Sections (Insights, Changes, To-Do)

Chapter Two: What Happened to My Little Princess?
Self-Awareness / Critical Judgment

So we have talked about what to expect on a macro level to understand hormones and friendships. But what is going on in your daughter's mind?

Well she has become more aware of what's going on outside of her and now she is questioning what's going on the inside. This reminds me of Eve and Adam in the Garden of Eden. After Eve and Adam ate the forbidden fruit, they were more aware of things (good and bad) going on around them and then became critical of the outside world through contrast and comparison relative to them. They know that they were naked and so covered themselves up with fig leaves.

This is no different than when your daughter was an infant, a toddler, and up into tweenhood (seven to twelve years old) when she is be**tween** a little child and a teen. She was invincible. She only cared about things going on in her world that affected her, and could do anything because she cared less about what you or others thought of her, she wasn't self-aware and comparing herself to the outside world. This was the age of innocence, a sort of naïveté.

Comparison and Confidence Shaken

So when she is aware of herself, she is also aware of others and how she measures up. She starts looking around and comparing herself to friends, enemies, frienemies (friends that vacillate between friends and enemies who don't really want her to succeed and / or she doesn't want the best for them either), and even stars / entertainers / and others in the spotlight.

At this time, she wants to be included and to only stand out for things that make people like her popular. She's afraid of not fitting in, sticking out like a sore thumb, people laughing at her, and failing. Don't we all just want to be liked / loved?

All kids go through this process, especially interracial kids that don't comfortably fit in one category. So what should you do?

> *Step 1: Acknowledge.* Empathize with her feelings. Let her know that many of her friends are experiencing the same lack of confidence. Some respond differently to this lack of confidence (become withdrawn / shy, try to overcome by being the center of attention, or just be in the middle of the road and go with the flow). Whatever her personality and coping mechanism, tell her that these feelings are normal (if they fall into what is considered normal). Abnormal activity is when she wants to harm herself or others or becoming depressed where it interferes with daily living activities. Check out chapter seven: Coping Mechanisms if you believe that your daughter's experience is abnormal with frequent episodes.

> *Step 2: Remind her.* Fear happens that's it. Point blank. Let her know that she has to try to be herself in order to be successful. Whatever being herself entails she should be her; this assumes that most of her activities are legal and productive. Of course, there will be failures, but experimentation of who you are and what you want to be is how you learn and grow.

> *Step 3: Reassure.* Tell her that she is beautiful in every way, inside and out, intelligent, and capable of being and doing anything that she wants. Okay she may be in this awkward ugly duckling stage, but we all go through that stage and come out beautiful on the other end. Tell her it is okay to be fearful of being unique, but it is *not* okay to let fear paralyze you from being the individual that you are, acting the way you want, and going after what you want. Yes, fear happens at all stages of life including adulthood. You may want to share instances of fear that you or others had when you were in high school (you have

to meet her where she is or she can't hear you) and how it turned out – favorable or not. Examples are the best way to show. Ask her what she thinks of the situation, if this is happening today, and what would she or her friends do differently or the same.

Step 4: Reinforce. We sometimes forget when we hear something only once or there is no action around it. Tell her often and show her by introducing her as my "Beautiful Daughter" who I am so proud of. Speak life and positive things in her life. If she wants to be a dancer, speak to her as such. Hi beautiful dancer! Let her know that she is loved and that she has the right to be loved.

Step 5: Challenge. Challenge her to be herself and confident in the person that she is today and the person she will become tomorrow. She is an original and no one can do her better so she should be the best she (whoever that is) that she can be.

Step 6: Be there. She will have days when no matter what you say, someone in the outside world will crush the reality and foundation that you, your family and community have built for her. Listen and empathize. Tell her that it will get better and to put it all in prospective. Remind her as Former First Lady Eleanor Roosevelt said, "No one can make you feel inferior without your consent."

A Teen Moment: "This stage of my life is when I started caring more and more about what other people thought and feeling like I needed to impress everyone else."

Notes Sections (Insights, Changes, To-Do)

_____

_____

_____

_____

_____

_____

_____

_____

_____

_____

_____

_____

_____

_____

_____

_____

_____

_____

_____

_____

_____

_____

Chapter Three: Pushing Boundaries

So your princess has decided to push the envelope and express her individuality. This could be a difficult time for both of you especially if she pushes *real* hard and if her idea of boundaries contrasts drastically from yours. Remember that this is a test where she determines her limits and yours. Her goal is to expand her boundaries as much as possible or even erase the lines so that you have no reign of control.

Your goal during this time, which is frequently tumultuous, is to allow her to express and explore her independence in a safe and nurturing environment that you provide while under your watchful eye.

Will Power - Independence or Disrespect?

When those hormones kick in, they can be murderous on your relationship with her. So what should you expect?

Well, she will now want to spend more "me time" in her room and or be with her friends. She will be mostly engaged with herself and others through music, books, and social media on any screen that she can get her hand on whether that be a computer or a smart phone. She may start saying what is hers (sounds familiar to our toddler saying "MINE, MINE") and where the lines are drawn. For instance she will start closing the door to her room and putting up a line on where her privacy begins. She may also have her mp3 player and or her smart phone on during car rides, dinner, and even conversations with you - How dare she!

She could also want to spend more time with her friends at your home (how lucky would that be for you?) or another place away from your watchful eye. It is a privilege if you have the "fun" house where kids congregate; this allows you to see their relationship dynamics.

And of course, she wants you to pay for all of her activities even if she works because let's face it — what's yours is hers and what's hers is hers according to her.

Additionally, her attitude changes where she believes she is your equal because let's face it — she is a teenager, an adult, and self-sufficient in her head, right? She may start flexing her muscles and challenging you on your decisions because it is no way in H – E – L – L, that you have ever been a teen and can understand her plight. If you are lucky, she challenges you respectfully, but sometimes you won't be that lucky.

She may also challenge her siblings and anyone in authority roles like teachers, sport instructors / coaches, and even her friends. So what should you do?

> *Step 1: Set expectations and rules of engagements.* Let her know that you know that she is growing up. With the growth comes expectations of:
>
> - **_Responsibility_**: Maybe her responsibilities include getting homework and chores done. She is a part of your family community and has to be a productive citizen. Some families require their teen to work to pay for that extraordinary smart phone, clothes, gas for driving the car, or extracurricular activity that she *must* have or even contribute to paying a small family bill. Others consider their daughter's job is to be a full time student.
>
> - **_Communication_**: Whether you set up a weekly discussion on Friday or dinner discussions every night, you and the family need to determine what is right for you when it comes to conversing. She also needs to know that she can come to you with anything.

And if she can't talk to you about a certain topic, then have her seek out a trusted and agreed upon aunt, uncle, teacher, or someone else that has morals like you that she can talk to. Even if you have chosen someone else for her to broach tough subjects with, you still need to have regular communication. Of course her best bet is to talk with you. Scheduling these talks informally (you can talk when you both are in the car) or formally is a must and will lay the groundwork for tough talks later on so start early and frequently and not just when there is an issue.

- **_Respect_**: There is a certain tone and demeanor that is required when communicating or engaging with peers, adults, and you. You must set this example when interacting with others so that she can follow. Just remember that she is still your child on the precipice of womanhood so she should be allowed to voice her opinion in ways that do not disrespect, wrongly accuse, threaten, or are not condescending to you or someone else.

Remind her that different relationships require different levels of respect. For example, she should engage differently with her peers than she would her teacher. And the way she interacts / acts will have reactions and consequences. Is she willing to live with the potential consequences of her actions?

Step 2: Expand her boundaries. Let's face it. She's not two or eight years old. So sit down with her and talk through the following with her:

- **_Time with friends_**: Encourage real time with friends as in the same room / space as another person. Not on instant messaging or social media, but the old fashion way of engaging with a person one on one. This time with friends also includes boyfriends, too (are you ready for this?)

- **_Screen time:_** How much time on a weekly basis should she engage with a screen, whether it is through television, handheld devices, smart phones, computers, games, etc.? Limiting screen time is important because it can take time away from important things like studying, reading, extracurricular activities, etc.

- _**Car time**_: If she is lucky enough to have access to a car when she is of driving age, then determine when and if she can drive with you or alone or ride with friends. Even if she is not driving, remember that some of her friends will be, so you need to establish her boundaries with them, too.

- _**Money spent**_: Do you provide an allowance? If not, maybe you should. This will help teach her financial responsibility and how to prioritize. Determine how much she gets and what the funds should be spent on. Also determine what you will pay for (school lunch and clothes, etc.) and what she pays for (movies, extra clothes, downloads, etc.).

**Step 3: Check up on her**. She is still your child no matter how mature she acts. Therefore, you need to check in with her to see if she is doing what you expect (tracking her phone is an option), to see if she is where she claims to be (calling her friend's parents), and is being truthful. Don't think of this as being a tough cop, but as being a responsible parent. Your job is to protect and provide and this is what you are doing by trusting _and_ confirming. Just make sure you are not so strict on her that she isn't allowed to make some mistakes with reasonable risks. If she isn't allowed to make some choices (good or bad), then she will not understand how to make decisions, the consequences of her actions, and how to become a rational, productive adult. Once she gains your trust after confirmation, then you can reduce the frequency or eliminate this step altogether.

**Step 4: Reward or Punish**. So we can hope that she remains 100% perfect. Whether she stays true to your expectations or veers off, you need to set up a reward or punishment to reinforce the behavior that you desire. The keys to this system are 1) rules need to outline what garners a reward or punishment 2) the reward or punishment should be customized to your daughter so that it matters enough to influence her behavior 3) you have to follow through on executing the reward or punishment. Be clear when you execute that you tell her - what she has done, why it deserves the reward or punishment, the expectations for next time, and how long that punishment or reward will last.

Step 5: Repeat steps 1-5. This method is an iterative process because as she matures and becomes more self-sufficient, the rules should change to allow more or less freedom and different reward systems as her dislikes and likes change.

This chapter is a guideline that you, your family, and your teen daughter must figure out to determine what works for you and your daughter and how much input you want her to have. Remember it is a privilege and not a right that your daughter participates in these guidelines so adjust her participation based on her behavior.

This section is a life-long lesson about interactions with people. This valuable lesson will bode well for her after high school and teach her how not only to deal with people in the workplace, but also her boyfriend or significant other. Remind her to walk a mile in another's shoes to get their perspective. Like you are setting up guidelines for respect and expectations, she will learn how to do the same for her relationships.

A Teen Moment: "In my early/mid teen years, I felt as if my mother was fighting me on everything. Most things I did or wanted to do were wrong or not ok in her eyes. There were times where I believe my mother honestly didn't love or want me. After I graduated high school, things completely changed. Now, I can't get enough of my mother. I'm beginning to realize in my late teen years that the things she said and did were attempts to mold me into a decent, respectable person."

A Teen Moment: "With my parents, I struggled with doing what they asked of me. I went through a short defiant phase."

Notes Sections (Insights, Changes, To-Do)

Chapter Four: The Mother / Daughter Debate
Yesterday You Were Right, Today So Wrong

As the first female model in your daughter's life, your relationship morphs as you both age. Before teenagehood, your daughter probably thought that you hung the sun and the moon. But once she became aware of herself, she also became aware of you and your faults. So what should you do with this individual who now critiques you, and sometimes so harshly?

> *Step 1: Don't take it personally.* It really is more about the issues that she sees with herself and the world around her. Some remarks or actions may seem hurtful; just remember that this is not about you.

> *Step 2: Allow her to have opinions respectfully.* She should be able to challenge you, if she does so respectfully. By respect, this means that she still holds your position of parent in high regard and does not try to take this coveted position. Remember, as a parent, you want her to grow as an individual, but the only problem with this is when she forgets that you and she *are not* equals.

> *Step 3: Remind her that you are the parent.* As the parent you may allow her the freedom of speech, but can also take it away from her at a moment's notice. She needs to be aware that although you communicate with her and allow her to have an opinion, that you *are not* friends. This may come later *after* you have raised her, but for now your first job is parent.

Mother's Roles

There are some relationships where a father or mother figure is not present. Then the situation becomes more difficult, but very doable. This means the mother / father who is present has to do both roles or preferably reach out to the *trusted* community of family and friends of the same sex of the missing parent to supplement. This surrogate could be an aunt, uncle, grandmother, grandfather, big brother, and big sister, etc. The other relationship setup is not as ideal as the mother / father combination, but can be just as successful given the number of single parent homes that produce good and great, productive daughters.

So what is your role as the mother?

Role 1: Model. Exhibit behaviors that you want her to demonstrate. You should display this exemplary behavior in all of your relations whether that's with your husband (or significant other), other children, family, and friends. Laying that foundation for her now should give her a good example to follow. You may not see the fruit of your labor today because raising a daughter is not a sprint, but a marathon. So continue to plant the seeds of good examples. Will you make mistakes sometimes? Sure you will, because you are human. Just try to make most of your interactions with her positive ones. Does that mean that eighty percent of the time you will have positive interactions? No, but the ratio should definitely be better than fifty-fifty.

Role 2: Monitor. Monitor her behavior and actions. So there are many ways to check in on her like having her text you when she arrives at the destination or have her take a picture of that person and text it to you to prove that she is where she says she is. You can also have her call from the location where she claims to be. Again, this shows you *trust* her to do the right thing, but will also *confirm* that she is doing so. I caution you to not use these drastic measures of tracking devices on her phone, car, etc. all the time *unless* she has lost your trust. Ultimately, you want to give her a chance to regain your trust if she lost it so you can slowly, but surely release stringent monitoring activities for less invasive ones.

Role 3: *Ruler*. So who is the parent here? You are. So that means you should behave as one. This means that your authority along with your spouse (or significant other) should lay down the law. You can allow your daughter to be a part of making the rules. This shows that you respect that she is growing up and has opinions. Ultimately, it is your call on what the final rules are for your household. Remember to have positive and negative consequences for the rules and to express them verbally and have her repeat them to you so there is no confusion regarding expectations. You may also want to write them down so there are no discrepancies of understanding between you and your daughter.

Role 4: *Enforcer*. Sometimes you just wish your daughter would follow the rules. And believe it, she will test her boundaries and break the rules sometimes. When she does, you have to enforce or reenforce the rules and their consequences. If you allow her to get away with things, then you really don't enforce your rules and she knows it. If that happens, she will continue with the behavior that you dislike. Also note, that the rules will need to change as she matures because things that worked yesterday won't work today and because her likes and dislikes change and so should the reward and punishment system.

Role 5: *Lifter*. Life has its moments when things are going well or not. The key here is for your daughter to learn how to respond to both the pleasant and unpleasant episodes that life throws not only her (she will believe that it is only her). Reassure her that others experience these things as well. When she has those bad days, just let her know that this too shall pass and tomorrow or next month this issue won't seem so inflated. Lift her spirits, her emotions, and self worth as often as you can.

Role 6: Cheerleader. As a part of Team_____ (insert your daughter's name here), you should be her biggest cheerleader. Providing her with encouragement to try different things especially those outside of her comfort zone. Just like with finding her circle of friends, she will need to experiment responsibly. Be there for her. This trait is particularly key with mothers because most of you have the natural propensity to nurture. Cheer her on.

A Teen Moment: "My mom and I have always been close but as I've gotten older I feel like we've gotten much closer. I never went through a stage like most teenage girls where they're constantly fighting with their mom. I was a complete momma's girl and her approval was the most important thing to me."

A Teen Moment: "Before teenage years, my mommy and I were best friends. During teenage years I constantly wanted to be the boss of my life. So because I wanted to be the only instruction I listened to, there was a constant battle for power between my mom and me."

Notes Sections (Insights, Changes, To-Do)

_____

_____

_____

_____

_____

_____

_____

_____

_____

_____

_____

_____

_____

_____

_____

_____

_____

_____

_____

_____

Chapter Five: Daddy Dearest
Father's Role

You will see that there are similarities between a mother and a father's role. These similarities are useful, especially when one of the parents is absent from your daughter's life or does not provide an example of an effective role model. However, even though the roles of the father have similar categories as the mother, there are distinguishable differences that are paramount because of the female / male relationship.

> **Role 1: Protector.** In most societies and families, the male figure provides the protection in relationships. This phenomenon rings true between the father and his child especially if it is a girl. So how does a father protect? He does the day to day physical protection of keeping harmful objects out of the way just like Mom, but he also gives the emotional support that provides a foundation for a sense of security. As your daughter ages, she still requires physical protection, but the emotional grounding becomes more important because it can protect her from others (sibling, classmate, friend, enemy, or even herself) who want to break her down emotionally. Protecting her from negative thoughts and actions.

> **Role 2: Mediator.** As you will see, this role is not found in the mother's category. This is because usually a mother and a daughter's relationship is adversarial and there needs to be a third party that can break the tie. So for a father, he should realize that the mother / daughter relationship may pit two females against each other. So what is a father to do?

- ***Talk with Mom first***: In a perfect situation (how many of those *really* exist?), the father and mother bond together and discuss differences of opinions and how to handle situations and issues before making decisions especially big ones regarding the daughter. Because life goes by so fast, many times you haven't had a chance to confer. So when that happens, tell your daughter that you need to talk with Mom first. If the daughter puts you on the spot and says she needs an answer immediately, then tell her that you need time before making a decision and for future reference she will need to come to you a certain amount of time (whatever time is best for you and your wife/her mother say twenty-four to seventy-two hours) before she would like to have your decision.

- ***Side with Mother:*** Daughters are notorious for dividing the forces that be (mother and father) by separately talking to one or the other and presenting her case and getting the parent at the time on her side. You can't fault her, right? You taught her to be smart and she's utilizing that skill set. The key is that you should realize what is going on and side with Mom or at least not side with the daughter behind the Mom's back. The father should rarely side with the daughter unless he and the mother agree beforehand that this is the route or united front that they will have.

- ***Challenge Daughter***: Remind her that there are always two sides and that she should think of her mother's viewpoint. For example, these are some type of questions you may pose to your daughter - What are mother's concern, why is she doing this, is mother intentionally trying to hurt or protect you?

- ***Require respect:*** Sometimes people have to agree to disagree when it's difficult to come to a consensus. Even if she disagrees with mother, the daughter must respectfully voice her concerns, but realize at the end of the day her mother's rules (which are also yours) are final.

Role 3: Enforcer. Why is the father always seen as the enforcer? Usually because the male figure has a low, authoritative voice, as compared to mom, that commands fear and respect. It is a tendency of the mom to be a nurturer and a father to be a disciplinarian. So following that train of thought, the father should enforce the rules and consequences laid out by he and mom and reinforce what mom says. This action stops the divide and conquer tactic that the daughter may use.

Role 4: Lifter (same as with Mother). Life has its moments when things are going well or not so much. The key here is for your daughter to learn how to respond to both the pleasant and unpleasant episodes that life throws not only her (she will believe that it is only her), but others too. When she has those bad days, just let her know that this too shall pass and tomorrow or next month this issue won't seem so inflated. Lift her spirits, her emotions, and self-worth as often as you can.

Role 5: Model. As the first male figure in her life, you are the role model for other males that she will encounter. No pressure, right? Well, actual there is pressure. Pressure for you to treat her mother right, so she has an example of a healthy relationship regardless of whether you and her mother are still together. Additionally, you need to treat your daughter respectfully like the young lady that she is becoming, but from a parental point of view. After all, she is still your daughter who you have authority over, but she is growing into a young lady who has opinions of her own, that should be heard. How do you want your daughter's significant other to treat her? If you yell at her, then she will think that this is appropriate behavior. Yet, if you chastise her respectfully, communicate with her on your expectations, and treat her well, then she will demand that from her boyfriend and husband in the future. A child relates better if you show her how it's done rather than tell her how and then give her an example that is different than what you say. Seeing is believing.

As Peggy O'Mara says, "the way we talk to our children becomes their inner voice", (O'Mara, www.TheSilverPen.com, www.pinterest.com, November 2012)." So let our words be directive and kind so that she hears a positive recording about herself.

A Teen Moment: "My dad was sort of like my best friend during my mid teen years. He was cool and outgoing. I believe he started talking with other parents and one day became really protective and asked a lot of questions. I don't feel as close to him anymore."

A Teen Moment: "My dad and I have always bonded over soccer and as I grew up and became a teenager my priorities shifted to boys and friends and I think it was really kind of hard on my dad because I was growing up so fast. I'll never forget my very last soccer game before I went to college my dad was tearing up and it was one of the first times I've ever seen him even show emotion. I think that really tells you a lot about our relationship."

A Teen Moment: "I've always had sports as a common ground with my dad. My relationship with my dad wasn't impacted by my teen years until later in high school when I decided I wanted to quit soccer. I felt like I was missing out on too much by having to attend practices, games, and tournaments. He was extremely frustrated and disappointed with my decision and this hurt our relationship. Looking back, I wish I would have listened to him. Quitting soccer is one of my biggest life regrets."

Notes Sections (Insights, Changes, To-Do)

_____

_____

_____

_____

_____

_____

_____

_____

_____

_____

_____

_____

_____

_____

_____

_____

_____

_____

_____

_____

Chapter Six: The Teen Daughter's Perspective

Some of the information found in this chapter may feel like a repeat of previous information because there is some overlap. However, the difference in this chapter is based on the perspective of girls who are current or recent teens .

Self-Image:

For the most part, teen daughters are very self critical and feel that they have inadequancies that need to be improved upon. Girls want to be like the popular, rich, cute / pretty, academic, beautiful teen girls in their circle of friends and / or like the rich and famous popular teens or young adults. With the prevalence of media especially the internet and other Social Media, your teen daughter constantly has ever changing images to compare and contrast herself to and inspire to be. She may value her self worth based on the number of friends she has or how popular she is. So what should you do?

> *Step 1: Empathize.* It is a very big deal to empathize with her and understand her feelings about wanting to be like someone else who seems to have it all. Who wouldn't be?

> *Step 2: Embrace Uniqueness.* Remind her that everyone is unique and has characteristics whether external (physical) or internal (emotions, academic, etc.) that are positive. Her deal is to understand her uniqueness, embrace it, and celebrate it. She needs to be comfortable in her own skin. Once she embraces herself and confidently

shows the world that she does, then others will follow suit and treat her accordingly.

Step 3: It's How You Finish. Remind her that circumstances tell her starting point, but not her finish line. So people who are popular or "in" today won't necessarily be that way or even successful tomorrow or in the future which also includes her. Bottom line is that she has the opportunity to change into whatever she wants to become.

A Teen Moment: "Just because the other person looks like she is okay doesn't mean that she is ; i.e Paris Hilton, Michael Jackson's daughter (Paris), Blake Lively (Gossip Girl), Lauren Conrad (The Hills)."

Friends Today

Most teens want to belong to a group. So your daughter may do or consider doing anything to fit in including having the right clothes, accessories, car, friends, etc. Your daughter may feel that if she and a friend are no longer friends because of diverging interests, a disagreement, or something else, she has failed and that she will never find another friend or group of friends to replace what she lost. So what should you do?

Step 1: A Moment in Time.

A Teen Moment: "Remind her that this (moment, feeling) is so trivial and that this will pass; it is not that important."

Step 2: Friendships Change. As stated earlier, let her know that friendships change as people do. Some friends will grow old with her while many others will only have a place in her life for a season.

A Teen Moment: "I had issues determining who were my real friends."

Step 3: Empathize. Emphathize with her about her pain, but let her know that this change in friendship status, whether this be with a girlfriend or a boyfriend, is a natural process that we all go through and that life continues to go on. Have her recognize and state what she is feeling and why and then ask what she would have wanted to change if she had a magic wand.

Step 4: Accept and Learn. Then ask her to release any negative thoughts and accept the things she can't change and change the things she can. Look for the lesson in any event and use this learning for the future.

Mother is a Pain

"Mom is so clueless. Mom is old fashion so she just doesn't get the new styles, fads, or music. How does she possibly understand what I am going through? Her examples are so from the past and are worthless today. She can't even comprehend my situation and struggles." So what you should you do?

Step 1: Mom Really Knows. Remind her that although technology has sped up communication with people, that relationships are fundamentally the same. So mom's experience from yesterday is still applicable today.

A Teen Moment… "Share a personal story because it makes you relatable."

Step 2: Remind Her. Remind your daughter that styles and fads fade and usually come around again. So many of the styles she likes today are things mom or others in her generation wore. Nothing is entirely new under the sun.

Step 3: Let Her Experiment. Mom should allow her to experience new things that won't hurt her. Let your daughter be an individual because she may think your ideas are old and antiquated. If she wises up, she may just realize that you have a trove of foundational advice that can help her thrive and navigate the teenage world and even a vintage closet that can inspire looks to die for.

Your teenage daughter also wants you to stay out of her business because she knows how to handle things. (Does she seriously think this? Of course she does!) However, when something goes wrong in her world, she wants mom to be on her side no matter what. Especially when your daughter thinks everyone is coming against her like dad, friends, and teachers, too. So what should you do, mom?

Step 4: Be there. Let her know that you will always be there for her and you want nothing but the best, but as a parent you must protect, guide, and direct her and provide insight that may be contrary to what she thinks. Mother knows best. ☺

Father is strict

Teen daughters already have extreme emotions so it shouldn't surprise you that father is either a source of extreme love or hate for her. If the father is a source of love, you are a blessed soul. Whether it's love or hate your daughter feels for her father, some antagonist perspectives on dear old dad is that he is a roadblock to having fun, his rules are so confining and he is selfish. Father says no to staying out late and going out with boys.

A Teen Moment: "Fathers don't understand being a girl. They are so clueless. Like when a girl cries about a boyfriend, he doesn't get it. And because he was a boy before, he knows more the intention of teenage boys. And when a girl is upset she should not be talking to her dad as much because he doesn't understand her emotional state or well being."

A Teen Moment: "he should explain that he was a teenage boy and he knows that his rules come out from a want to protect the *girl and not just to be a party pooper. When he explained himself, then it made more sense to the girls.*

Boys, Boys, Boys…

Why do girls want or need boys?

Reason 1: Complete Them.

*A Teen Moment "Boys **complete them** and (girls don't feel) they're a successful girl until they have a boyfriend. Then these girls can't develop their own identity outside of the boy. They need to be strong individuals to understand boys."* So what can parents do?

- ***Maintain a healthy relationship*:**

A Teen Moment: "If your daughter witnesses her mother putting up with disrespectful behaviors, then she doesn't know that she doesn't have to."

Moms and fathers should respect each other whether they are together or not. The parents' relationship is a foundation for what should and shouldn't happen and what is considered healthy.

Reason 2: Status / Elevate.

*A Teen Moment: "Boys **elevate** their (your daughter's) status and she will likely do anything that he asks for popularity."*

Reason 3: Love Them.

*A Teen Moment: "They (teen girls) reach out to boys to **show endearing love** especially if they did not receive the* *love at home. Many don't have a strong male presence and so they look for a boy to be their "father figure" to tell them what to do."*

Reason 4: For Attention.

A Teen Moment: "Boys are so foreign and different at this point in time, girls **want their attention** *since they don't understand them. Meanwhile boys haven't even made their transition into adulthood so they barely notice us. None of us NEED boys though.* So what can parents do?

• ___Show her love___:

A Teen Moment: "But you need to show your daughter physically and emotionally that you love her so she won't feel the need to go outside to "find that love" to complete her.

Reason 5: Peer Pressure.

A Teen Moment: "It is the influence of people around you that makes you feel like you need a boyfriend. Once you have that first boyfriend is when you begin to feel what it's like to love."

A Teen Moment: "I fell into a lot of peer pressure as a teen. I always dated someone older than me and that had a huge impact on feeling like I needed to be a part of their parties and activities. This led to a lot of sneaking out and lying to my parents."

A Teen Moment: "Growing up with parents that were so perfect for each other I feel like I've always really wanted something like what they have and that's made me a relationship kind of girl. Since fifth grade I've constantly had a boyfriend and I think it's my way of trying to find the person who I'm going to end up with for the rest of my life. Looking back at high school I feel like everyone had boyfriends and for me it was comforting to have that one person who I knew cared about me in a different way than anyone else. I always tell my parents that they've set the standard pretty high."

Dating boys can be a rewarding and fulfilling experience as long as she knows the proper relational expectations from both she and him.

Notes Sections (Insights, Changes, To-Do)

So there will be trying times for your daughter that are really important to her today, but won't be in the grand scheme of life. These times will require navigation by you, but more importantly by her. If she manages these times well, she will have the foundation to navigate life's obstacles that have higher stakes, risk, and rewards. When these situations arise, you may want to step in and save her, but you can't. You can only help her navigate. It's like when you helped her memorize her time tables; you provided that support and gave her special techniques to remember. But, you couldn't take the test for her. You can only hold her hand so much and walk with her so far into the schoolyard of life.

So fast forward to her teen years. Regardless of the situation, your daughter needs to learn how to cope in the classroom of life. She must learn this coping skill on her own. You can't give her this skill or buy her happiness. It has to come from within and has to be learned. So what can you do? You can provide navigation tools for her to try, analyze, digest, learn from, or dismiss since you used to know her well, right? She may have changed some, but fundamentally her likes may be the same.

ACTIVITY PAUSE

She can use a diversion technique of participating in something that makes her feel well and or think highly of herself.

1. Physical activities: She can burn energy by playing a sport, a musical instrument, dancing, or whatever makes her happy. She can take a walk around the block (of course during a safe hour) by her-self, with her pet, or with someone she cares about that cares about her.

*2. **Setting the mood:*** She can listen to music, light candles, and just relax.

*3. **Retreat or Escape:*** She can take a nap, read a book, or do a creative activity like writing or poetry. That's what Taylor Swift did. ☺ Your daughter can release the negative energy and increase her endorphins by doing something alone in a private moment or with others.

Doing any of these activities cause her to take a pause or a break from the thing that is pulling her down. Usually when she takes a break, it may force her to look at the situation differently with a new perspective so she realizes that this will pass, it's not so bad, or she could come up with another solution on her own.

COMMUNICATION

Communication is key as mentioned in **Chapter Three: Pushing Boundaries**. To refresh your memory, you should review that sec-tion, but also read this section since it provides a similar, but different perspective on communication and coping.

*1. **Talking it out.*** As you know, sometimes your daughter won't open up. You should take every opportunity to talk to her. It doesn't have to be anything formal like at six in the evening on Sunday, but it has to be consistent. Set the mood in an informal, non-threatening environment. Perhaps you can talk to her when you are riding in the car (you may have to separate her from the cell phone and stop her from texting or engaging in social media), shopping, riding a bike, or even having dinner. It's better if she talks to you or her dad, but she can also talk to others.

She can talk to a BFF (Best Friend Forever or at least Today - BFT). And if she is blessed enough to have siblings or first cousins that she is close to, have her reach out to them. If she doesn't want to do that, you may have her sibling call her or the parents of the cousins hint around for their child to call your child. Sometimes she won't say anything and she may just need a hug, a kiss, or a kind word. Be a constant in her life. Although, she may push you away, continue to come in and talk to her. Let her know that the things that she is experiencing today seem really big in her life and are right now, but will grow smaller in her life as grander more important things occur.

2. Talking to a professional: Sometimes she gets to a point where she won't talk to you or anyone else. To keep the lines of communication open, she can talk to a religious leader, a school counselor, or a therapist. Just know that depending on the laws in your state that your daughter's talks with a psychologist (an academic doctor with a Ph. D – a doctorate of philosophy) or a psychiatrist (a medical doctor) can be confidential and won't be required by law to be shared with you unless something is revealed that shows that she could be harmful to herself or others. Additionally, if she talks to a psychiatrist realize that their main tool in their "black bag" is medication that your daughter will take to alter her mental state to get back to what is accepted as "normal" teenage behavior.

Your daughter may or may not require this type of intervention, but realize that medicine will most likely be given by the psychiatrist. Your goal here is to understand if medicine is for your daughter, if so what are the side effects (suicide could be one), the treatment plan, and the exit strategy (living with the meds for the rest of her life or the gradual weaning of the meds as a temporary fix.)

PRAYER, SPIRITUALITY

If you have a raised her to believe in God or a higher being, she can lean back on this great foundation. She can pray through these tough times, read the Bible, and meditate on clearing her mind and focusing on a better day. There is nothing new under the sun that she is experiencing today that did not occur in the Bible; albeit, the landscape and technology are different, which can cause current issues to be magnified to the world at a quicker pace. However, the core concerns and values remain. Whether there is hurt, hopelessness, bad times, fear, loss of a loved one, desperation, doom, anxiety, depression, and despair, the Bible speaks of those times and how real people made it through by believing and asking God for guidance and deliverance. Remind her that joy comes in the morning and the universe has a way of allowing people to reap good or bad efforts based on the type of deeds they sowed.

Step 1: Love. Faith. Hope. Also remind her that there is JOY, peace, happiness, and love, and she just needs love (from you her parents, friends, and others), faith (in herself and in God's way of handling things), and hope that tomorrow will be better.

Step 2: Bad & Good Happen. Tell her that bad and good things happen to both bad and good people so although her issues seem like it only happens to her - they don't.

Step 3: Positivity. It's all about her attitude and how she perceives and responds to the world. If she is positive, the world will give back positive things to her. Conversely, if she is negative, she will see the universe this way which could cause others to retreat from her thus alienating herself. Who wants to be around a Debby Downer?

Step 4: Temporary. Last, let her know that her hurt is temporary. And this too shall pass.

Step 5: Religion and Spirituality. And if you haven't raised her in this environment, it's not too late. If she is not familiar with religion or spirituality, she alone or with your help can reach out to a church / synagogue / temple / etc. where there are many people to guide her. From calling in and asking for help to attending service and finding a group or a community in the church, she can find someone there willing to help her cope. Priests, Pastors, Leaders, etc. are there to help her navigate this world based on religious knowledge and wisdom. It is best to find a place of worship that can use the faith based historical lessons and apply them to the life that she is living today.

VOLUNTEERING

Additionally, if she finds herself constantly thinking about her life and just how bad it is, she should start removing the focus from herself and help others in need. When she glimpses into other's life that is disadvantaged differently than hers, it may provide insights into how to deal with her life which now doesn't look so bad.

A Teen Moment: "Dancing was big part of my coping. Being good at something like I was in dance, this made me feel good and also gave me an outlet. Personal writing (not something that I shared with others) was also an outlet to express myself and work out my issues and validate my feelings... my changes."

A Teen Moment: "I'm not sure if I really coped. I held most things in and didn't do anything special to feel better."

A Teen Moment: "Talking things through has always been a huge coping mechanism for me. I talked some things out with my mom and the rest out with friends. If my sister had been older at the time I would have talked to her."

A Teen Moment: "When I look back, I think I just got through it. I think I did what I could to get through those years whether it was soccer, boyfriends, Prozac, or a therapist. I just wanted to be happy. Now that I think of it, soccer was definitely a great outlet for me. I enjoyed going away almost every weekend because it took me away from a lot of the stress that came with being a teenager. Obviously I hated missing out on things that my friends got to do but if I could do it again I wouldn't change a thing."

Notes Sections (Insights, Changes, To-Do)

Chapter Eight: Moving Forward and Looking Back

Moving Forward

First of all, congratulations on raising your teen daughter! This is not an easy feat to do well, but you have to do it. If not you, then whom? As a parent, your role is to protect and provide. And as long as you aid her in becoming a productive, independent woman while allowing her to make some minor, non-permanent mistakes on that journey, you have done your job! Just remember to savor these good and not so good times because this time comes only once and she will be grown before you know it. Keep moving forward. ☺

Looking Back

While you are going through this trying, yet wonderful time, realize that you aren't the first to make this journey. So commiserate using some advice and comments listed here from both parents and daughters that are going through this phase right now as well who have made it through. Take solace in these words of wisdom to know that you are not alone and that this too shall pass.

Parents in Their Own Words

Expectations: *As a current / past parent of a teen daughter, what did you expect during the teen years?*

- I expected mood swings…
- I expected her to decide on who she was and what kind of person she wanted to be. To demonstrate ambition and a kind of expectation and personal vision of what kind of life she wanted to live. Some identity problems and questions / issues. I expected her to kind of establish not really a lifestyle, but kind of a circle of friends.
- To actually love them (my daughters). Didn't realize they would push me away.
- Initially, I didn't know what to expect. Didn't realize it was going to change my life being a father. One thing that I expected was that each child was the same. I found out that every child is an individual and you raise them differently because of different personalities and that was a learning an experience.

Expectations: *As a current / past parent of a teen daughter, what didn't you expect during the teen years?*

- Their (two daughters) lack of confidence.
- As a divorced parent, I didn't expect that I wasn't going to get support from their mother (two teen daughters) and that I didn't have backing from my ex. I think it is easier for rules if both divorced parents are on the same page with rules. Had a lot of trouble with them in school. Communication should have been between ex-wife and me.
- Depression, academic struggles, self-identity issues, didn't expect the need to be liked by everybody.
- That I wouldn't be able to fix all of her problems and that I shouldn't fix them because part of being an adult is being independent and solving your own problems.

Best: What was / is the best thing about raising a teenager girl?

- The best is watching them grow into independent young women.
- They are at an age that they do communicate and you can talk to them, but rather or not they listen to your reasoning is another thing. The simple things like knowing that they are in the house. Having them around.
- Watching them grow into their own person; it's very rewarding to watch them turn into little adults.
- Seeing them grow and turn into an individual personality. Every one of my daughters had a love affair with animals. All of them had a fear of insects and spiders. Being able to watch them grow as a person and their loves and talents including the love for helping those who really need it.

Worst: What was / is the worst thing about raising a teenager girl?

- The worst is, having to stay one step ahead of them in order to allow them to make their own mistakes, but curb the major ones before they make them. The life changing ones are permanent.
- Harder things: knowing when to let go and when to pull back (when they need to fall) so then they learn. Seeing them struggle. Knowing that my girls are different and require different parenting. Knowing that when I step in they may get mad, but I know what's best.
- As a divorced parent, when they aren't near me and are at their mom's place.
- I think the best and worst thing about raising a teenager is seeing myself in her based on the parenting job I have done. I have managed to pass on some of my less attractive attributes as well as good ones but at least I can recognize it which helps me to correct the behavior inside me. I have learned some very valuable lessons raising my first teenager which is good since there are 3 more on her heels.

- Her having to learn as much on a hands on basis instead of not being able to accept guidance from people (parents) who have experienced it before. Watching her run into brick walls when she didn't have too.
- Seeing their pain and realizing that pain is necessary to grow.
- My first child was a daughter. My fear of when she became a teenager and that she would follow the wrong crowd, and then driving and her safety.

Teen Girls: In Their Own Words:

Changes: What changes (physical and emotional), did you notice when you became a teen?

- More responsibility, realized there was a consequence for every action because "sorry" won't be able to fix all of your mistakes.
- I was an independent person and my mistakes were my own. And my parents couldn't fix everything for me.
- My mother got stricter. Everything was looked at differently. All of sudden, I couldn't have guys in the bedroom. Parents want to think that you are still younger than you are. In my mother's mind, I hadn't changed.
- I noticed that I became very attached to the other teens in my life. I constantly wanted attention from my friends and significant others. Physically, I noticed that my body was looking like a grown woman and a lot of negative attention came with that.
- When my anxiety was bad, I couldn't really control my emotions and it really impacted a lot of my relationships. I grew up playing soccer so I've always been very fit with an athletic build. I noticed my weight really fluctuating, as I got older. I look back at pictures now and I call one period of time "my big stage" and then I have one point that I call "my entirely too skinny stage" which was my Junior year of high school which had a lot to do with my anxiety.
- Physical change was completely obvious and expected: boobs, acne, awkwardness, etc. But when it came to emotionally, I loss

a lot of my confidence and became hyper-sensitive. Gotta love being a girl.

Relationships: How did becoming a teen impact your relationship with your mother?

- Got into more fights, because of opposing views and different personalities.
- She still viewed me as a child and I wanted her to recognize my autonomy. I felt I wasn't a little girl and I wanted more privacy than I was given. We got in more fights because we were the same person. Living with yourself isn't fun.
- It pulled us away from each other and made us grow apart. Our opinions became opposing. It's hard because she is struggling to keep you young and you are struggling to be treated more like an adult.

How did becoming a teen impact your relationship with your father?

- Didn't change really, except we spent more time together because he wanted me to be able to come to him with my problems.
- I became distant from my father because he wasn't a girl. I didn't know how to talk to him. And even more so than my mother, he still views me more like a little girl and that is why we fought most of the time.
- My family has always been a close family but I never considered myself having a great relationship with my dad. Not that it was anything even close to bad I just considered my mother and me to be much closer. I think that had a lot to do with the fact that he was never home. He traveled for a living so I got used to not seeing him every day or talking to him every day. I was so used to him being gone. I think we missed out on a lot of one on one time which could have been beneficial to our relationship.
- Honestly becoming a teen didn't change my relationship between my dad and me because he treated me the exact same way

he did throughout my whole life. I expected the strictness and old school parenting values. Consistency is the reason for this.

How did becoming a teen impact your relationship with your friends?

- Got more picky with my friends because I knew what I wanted with people, was a lot more aware of who I became friends with. Chose friends – takes a long time to be friends with people so chose friends for a little while and then after a while if I didn't see a real friendship then would not be friends with them anymore.
- When I became a teen, I became more of individual and so I didn't have to hang out with anyone that I didn't want to. When you are a teen, you pick your friends and not your parents. My group of friends changed and it was hard because I was more self-conscious so it was hard for me to make friends.
- Becoming a teen, you noticed more of who was growing up and who wasn't quite ready to grow up. You became more opinionated and set in your ways. And everyone handled things more maturely than they would have previously.
- I often struggled with putting my relationships with boyfriends before my friends. This is something I regret deeply and would love to go back and change.
- I looked to my friends for advice but that wasn't smart because they were going through the same changes and making the same mistakes as me.

Issues: What issues did you have as a teenager with parents, friends, boys / significant others?

- Being completely truthful with my parents because I would be afraid they would tell me no so I would lie.
- I felt like I couldn't relate with my parents and so I wouldn't relate to them. I didn't realize until I was this age (18) how much

I appreciated them. With friends, I felt I had to impress them and then realizing I didn't have to impress them was a big part of growing up.

- Boys definitely don't grow up as fast as girls so they aren't on the same level as you are on many things. Parents still keep you under a bubble and try to push rules on you which most definitely become an issue and causes tension.

- Majority of my issues with just about everyone stemmed from my anxiety. It impacted the way I thought about everything and really put a strain on my relationships. I had trust issues with my boyfriend when I didn't have a reason too. I was always analyzing every little thing and thinking the worst. It's a little embarrassing but I used to cry because I thought my parents liked my sister better. If my boyfriend didn't want to hang out I automatically assumed that he didn't care about me. I know that's all very dramatic but I was really in a rough place and needed help.

- I went through a lot of different friend groups when I was a teenager and I think that's because I didn't really trust girls. I knew how mean they could be.

- I felt like absolutely no one understood me.

How did you cope as a teen girl?

- Didn't do much coping; I knew it would be over soon so it wasn't going to last forever.

- Dancing was big part. Being good at something like I was in dance, this made me feel good and also gave me an outlet. Personal writing (not something that I shared with others) was also an outlet to express myself and work out my issues and validate my feelings my changes.

- Shut out my mom and focused more on my friendships.

- I didn't. I wish I wrote more and didn't hold in all of my feelings of insecurity.

Were meds a part of your coping mechanism? Did your coping mechanism work?

- I have always suffered with anxiety but didn't start taking medicine until I was almost twenty. I often wonder if my teen years would have been different with the addition of medicine.
- Unfortunately yes, medicine was a part of my coping mechanism. My anxiety was pretty debilitating and affected not just my emotions but my relationships, my physical appearance, and my life. Prozac did absolute wonders for me and have made me a much happier person.
- Yes, they were. It did help. Therapy (talking) helped more. Medicating things don't always help, but helped as a temporary relief to get through the rough patches.
- No, I didn't use meds.
- I did take medication, I still take medication and for me, personally, it has worked. I do have many friends who were on medicine unnecessarily though.

What do you wish you could tell, or could have told your mother while going through these changes?

- I agree with the disciplining and things that they wouldn't let me do because now that I am in college I am responsible and have discipline.
- Wish I could have told her thanks a lot more and expressed my gratitude more frequently because I didn't know how to express myself. Kids are actually more appreciative than parents think.
- That she needs to let me experience things for myself.
- I wish I could tell my mom that I really wanted/needed to talk to her but at times I felt like I couldn't because I wasn't sure if she really liked me.
- I went through a really bad relationship when I was fifteen years old. I know my mom knows that it wasn't a good one but I don't think she ever knew how bad. I felt like I was in love and needed

to do everything he wanted me to do to make him happy. I was pressured into having sex and dealt with a lot of emotional abuse. I am still too ashamed to tell her to this day. I wish I had felt comfortable talking to her about this. It probably would have stopped the relationship from lasting so long.

- When I was at the lowest point in my life with my anxiety and how much weight I had lost from it, I wish I could have told my mom that there was nothing she could have done differently to change it. She was the support I needed.
- I need more freedom to make my own mistakes.

What do you wish you could / could have tell / told your father while going through these changes?

- I appreciate his protectiveness, but it didn't feel like it at the time. I wish I could tell him that I heard him and I understand; my life is better because of the lessons that he taught me.
- I wish I could tell my dad that it felt like something changed between us and I'm not sure what it was.
- I wish I could have explained to him exactly how I was feeling when I was going through everything with my anxiety. I always went to my mom because I knew she would be more understandable. Maybe if I told my dad more, we would've had a closer relationship when I was a teenager.
- I promise you, Dad, you have no clue what I'm going through. So because talking it out will be confusing and uncomfortable, I just need to know you're here for support.

Advice: What advice would you give future teen girls?

Teens:
- Parents are usually always right. And things get better. You may be miserable now, but everything that your parents are doing for you is right because they want what's best for you.
- Tell the teens that everything that is happening isn't as big as you think it is. If you do something embarrassing, people will forget

it. A lot of the things that you are feeling are in your head and not manifested in the real world or in your friends' minds.

- That although it is hard, try and find a balance between doing what you want to do and what you parents think you should do. Not to get caught up in the present and to remember that there is a future.

- I would advise teen girls to find people who actually care about them and be open with your parents. Also, I would tell girls to respect themselves and make decisions based on what they really want.

- I would tell future teen girls that no matter what, you have to be true to yourself and do what it is that makes you happy. As a teen you are too focused on what everyone else wants and thinks. I know it's easier said than done but you have to have respect for yourself and do what is best for you. Also, if you are fortunate enough to have great parents like I did, don't be afraid to talk to them. Despite what you may think, they will not judge you but instead support you more than you would expect. I would also tell them to never put boys before their friends. The boys will come and go but friends will be there throughout.

- ENJOY IT! I'm only twenty and I always think about how I don't want to grow up anymore and how much I miss being in high school. It will fly by!

- Confidence is key; that's what I've learned since I've gotten to college. If you know that you are the best thing in the room, opportunities will come to you. All girls feel uncomfortable with themselves right now, so know that what you're struggling with is no different from your friend's plights.

Parents:
- To seek their value from within and not from what others think of you. Know your worth.

- There are so many things that are fun that you can do while you are younger and have your health; do as many things as you can until you find what you like to do and then have a passion about it.

Give it your all. Don't go half ass it. Do the best you can at what you want to do.

- Don't be afraid to be yourself. The sooner you can be comfortable in being yourself the less pressure you will have to conform and compare.

What advice would you give parents about raising teen girls?

Teens

- You have to be open with your kids, kind, and listen to each other. You have to have open communication so both parents and teen daughters can tell each other things.
- Realize that it is very stressful to be a teenage girl and that we feel more pressure from peers and so you need to show affection and appreciation for your daughter more than you think you. Remind them that everything isn't as big of a deal as she thinks it is; do this without belittling their problems.
- Even though you want to protect your little daughter, you need to let her find out who she is and experience and create her own experiences.
- I would advise parents to be patient and try to get close to their daughter.
- Girls need their parents, especially their mom in my case, throughout the teen years.
- I would tell parents to strive to have as open a relationship as possible. I think it is so important that girls feel like they can go to their parents about anything and it be completely without judgment.
- I would tell them that spending time with them and making memories with them is *so* important. Having that one on one time together helps to reinforce the bond that is already formed and make it much stronger.
- We're difficult, we push you away, but we will ALWAYS love you. And if we don't realize everything you are doing for us now, we will soon.

Parents

- Finding the balance between knowing when you can be their friend and be their parent. Realizing the way that you were raised may not be successful or may need to be altered for your daughters. Raising your daughters differently than the way your parents raised you is okay.
- Be prepared for social upheaval. Always let them know that they can come home and home is a safe haven.
- As a parent you aren't going to be liked all the time and that's okay. Setting clear expectations and boundaries are a must.
- Don't be so strict, give your daughter a little bit of space. Tell her what is out there and prepare her for it, but loosen up the reins and let them experience some things and trust her unless she does otherwise. Let her know that there will be consequences for your actions. Give them flexibility to make their own mistakes. Being too strict will make them rebel and be wild when they are away from you.
- Ease up a bit, have grounded expectations (for your daughter) and stand up for them *but* understand that she is going through major changes - physically and emotionally. That too will pass. Relax and go with the flow. Go with the basics and make sure the values are met. Don't push things (so far) that you become enemies. Keep her grounded in rules based on family values and your religious beliefs. Don't give up on her or the educational expectations that you have. Basically, teens want to please their parents. Little things like dressing in strange manners – don't get up tight about it; it is just a way to express themselves.

Best and Worst

What is the best thing about being a teenage girl?

- Being able to see yourself grow into a mature young lady.

- Not having as much responsibility. I liked being cared for by my parents and having freedom to be an adult.
- You are experiencing new things.
- I like this stage in my life because I'm still young enough to be care free sometimes. I feel special being a teenage girl in my major in college because some people feel that it's a man's field. Also, I love makeup, dresses, and pretty nails.
- It's a time for growth in so many ways. Opportunities to figure out who you are, are everywhere and some of the changes can be really exciting! Enjoy and embrace every moment because life is too short not to.
- Knowing that this is just the in-between stage, you're about to bloom into the most beautiful unique flower.

What is the worst thing about being a teenage girl?

- Having to learn lessons the hard way.
- Not knowing what you are doing. Learning terrible lessons because you didn't know.
- Very emotional period of your life and you go through a lot of changes in your lifestyle.
- For me, it's getting so emotionally attached to something or someone.
- The worst thing is just trying to figure out yourself. Who you are and what you like and not letting others influence you.
- Judgments from other insecure girls.

It Is Worth It

After all of the sleepless nights, stressful days, points of confusion, disappointment, worry, *it is worth it*. It is worth seeing your daughter:

- Grow, smile, love, mature, succeed, become her own person, graduate, help others, make good decisions, learn, teach others, lead, marry, and have kids of her own.

So when your little girl challenges you and goes through the awkward teenage years, just remember, that this metamorphism is a process. One that is necessary. A diamond like your daughter must undergo pressure before it achieves its final state of sparkle and shine. ☺ Happy parenting!

Notes Sections (Insights, Changes, To-Do)

Made in the USA
Middletown, DE
19 July 2020